Motivating Your Team Workbook

Why People Work

Jody Holland

OPENING QUOTE

"If you intentionally become less than you are capable of being, then I warn you, you will be unhappy for the rest of your life."

Abraham Maslow

CONTENTS

ACKNOWLEDGMENTS

I would like to acknowledge all of the leaders throughout the years that have shown me what works and what doesn't work in business. I have learned from the good, the bad, and the ugly. I am thankful for all of those experiences.

Learning Objectives

Create an awareness of the external and internal factors affecting employee performance

Understand your own motivation and what motivates others

Enhance your knowledge of various motivational theories

Apply these theories to the workplace

Expand your skills and your perspective

What Is Your Potential?

"If you deliberately become less than you are capable of being, then I warn you... you will be unhappy for the rest of your life."

--Abraham Maslow

What Has Been Observed?

Our research has shown that a motivated workforce...

- Is less likely to call in sick to work
- Is less likely to find ways to NOT perform their job
- Is more likely to help out their coworkers
- Is more likely to stay working for you (less turnover)
- And is more likely to find ways to contribute.

Question?

Why did you come to work today?

Are your reasons different than your employees' reasons?

Job Performance Has A Few Components

Job Performance equals

THE

KEYConcept

Developing Great People

Job Fit multiplied by

The Person's Ability To Do The Job multiplied by

The Person's Training multiplied by

The Person's Motivation

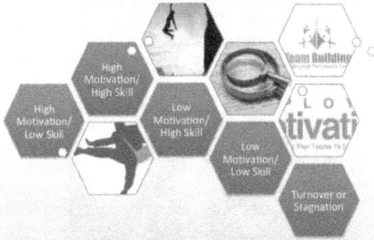

Life Cycle Of Employment Motivation

What Drives Us?

Intrinsic motivation flourishes in an environment where employees feel like they are a part of something bigger than themselves. People work for a purpose and a passion.

How Do We Motivate Long-Term?

Engage
- Employees must buy in to the organization and the leadership

Educate
- Employees must learn to carry out their job duties and have the right tools.

Empower
- Employees must be given the right culture, training, and leadership to grow and flourish.

Maslow's Hierarchy
Self-Actualization
Esteem
Belonging/Love
Safety & Security
Physiological

Clayton Alderfer's ERG Theory

Clayton P. Alderfer

ERG theory (Existence, Relatedness, and Growth), and was created to align Maslow's motivation theory more closely with empirical research.

G – R – E

G **Growth**
Self-Actualization
External Esteem Needs

R **Relatedness**
Internal Esteem Needs
Social Needs

E **Existence**
Safety Needs
Physiological Needs

How Alderfer Was Different

- Alderfers ERG theory demonstrates that <u>more than one need may motivate at the same time</u>. A lower motivator need not be substantially satisfied before one can move onto higher motivators.

- The ERG theory also accounts for differences in need preferences between cultures better than Maslow's Need Hierarchy; <u>the order of needs can be different for different people</u>. This flexibility accounts for a wider range of observed behaviors. For example, it can explain the "starving artist" who may place growth needs above those of existence.

- The ERG theory acknowledges that if a higher-order need is frustrated, <u>an individual may regress to increase the satisfaction of a lower-order need which appears easier to satisfy</u>. This is known as the *frustration-regression principle*.

Leadership Lessons Learned

- Managers must recognize that <u>an employee has multiple needs to satisfy simultaneously</u>. According to the ERG theory, leadership focused exclusively on one need at a time will not effectively motivate.

- The <u>frustration-regression principle impacts workplace motivation</u>. For example, if growth opportunities are not provided to employees, they may regress to relatedness needs, and socialize more with co-workers. Or, the inability of the environment or situation to satisfy a need for social interaction might increase the desire for more money or better working conditions. If Leadership is able to recognize these conditions, steps can be taken to satisfy the frustrated needs until the subordinate is able to pursue growth again.

Herzberg's Two-Factor Theory

Satisfiers

- Achievement
- Recognition
- Nature of Work
- Responsibility and Advancement

Dissatisfiers

- Company Policy
- Bad Administration
- Incompetent Supervisor
- Poor Working Conditions

Frederick Herzberg
(18 April 1923 – 19 January 2000)

"Father of job enrichment principle"

WWII Nazi Dachau Concentration Camp witness, Germany
1946 Graduate, City College
1950 Ph.D., University of Pittsburgh
1951 Research Director, Psychological Services of Pittsburgh
1957 Professor of Psychology, Case Western Reserve University, Cleveland
1972 Professor of Management, University of Utah

1959 book release:
"The Motivation to Work"
Focuses on a particular motivation theory which biased his future publications

1968 publication on motivation:
"One More Time,
How Do You Motivate Employees?"
- 1.2 million reprints in 1987
Most requested article from Harvard Business Review

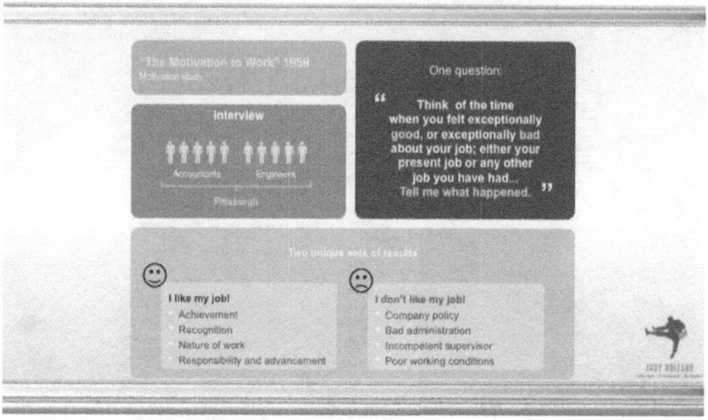
"The Motivation to Work" 1959
Motivation study
Interview
Accountants
Engineers
Pittsburgh
One question:
" Think of the time when you felt exceptionally good, or exceptionally bad about your job; either your present job or any other job you have had... Tell me what happened. "
Two unique sets of results
I like my job!
Achievement
Recognition
Nature of work
Responsibility and advancement
I don't like my job!
Company policy
Bad administration
Incompetent supervisor
Poor working conditions

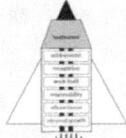

Two-factor motivation

Motivators
Job content

Promote

The absence of these conditions **doesn't necessarily dissatisfy**. But when present, they build strong levels of motivation that result in good job performance.

Hygiene factors
Job context

Improve

The presence of these conditions to the satisfaction of the employee **doesn't necessarily motivate**, but their absence results in dissatisfaction.

Hygiene factors are merely a launch pad - when damaged or undermined we have no platform, but in themselves they do not motivate. The contrast is true for motivators.

21

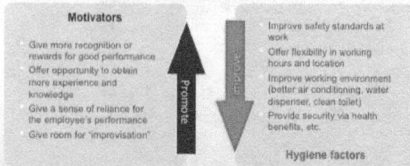

How to implement Hygiene-Motivator?

Implementation at different professions

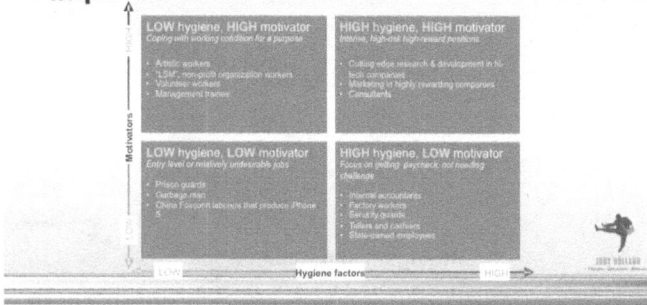

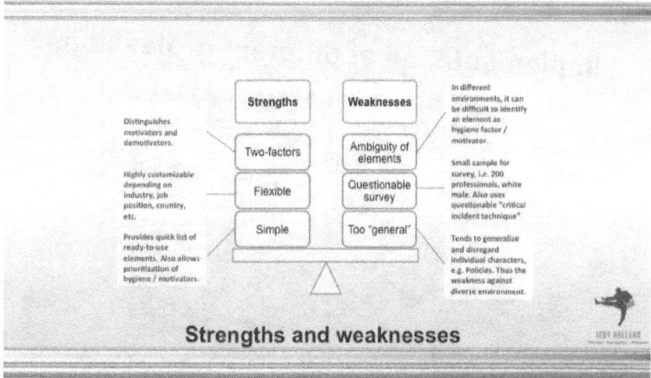

Strengths and weaknesses

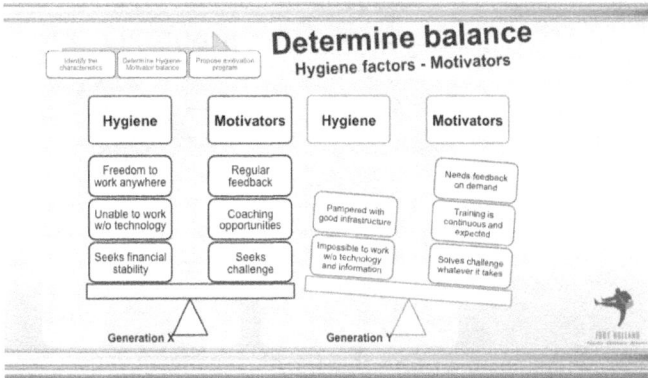

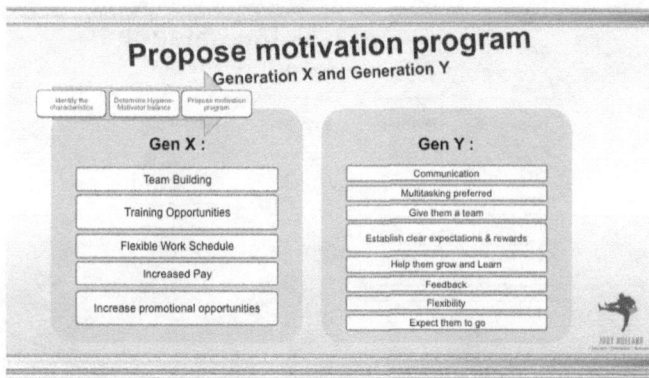

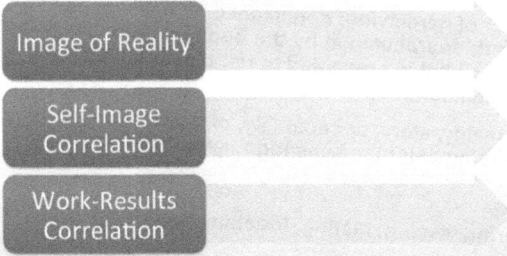

Holland's Theory of Values-Based Drive

- Image of Reality
- Self-Image Correlation
- Work-Results Correlation

Image and Perception

The act of perceiving; cognizance by the senses or intellect; apprehension by the bodily organs, or by the mind, of what is presented to us; discernment; apprehension; cognition.

The quality, state, or capability, of being affected by something external; sensation; sensibility.

(Hearing, seeing, tasting, touching, smelling)

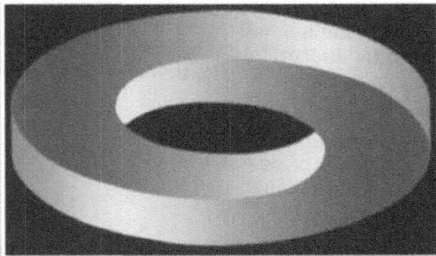

Apperception

Apperception means making sense of a new perception by interpreting it in terms of our existing concepts, languages, beliefs, theories and our past experiences.

Our mental encyclopedia of pre-existing concepts, beliefs, ideas, theories has traditionally been termed our *apperception mass*.

Source: Karl Jung's definition of apperception

Dan Pink – Drive

Autonomy
The desire to direct our own lives

Mastery
The desire to get better and better at something

Purpose
The yearning to do what we do in the service of something larger than ourselves

"We simply assume that the way we see things is the way they really are or the way they should be. And our attitudes and behaviors grow out of these assumptions."

~Stephen Covey~

WHAT DID YOU SEE?

Motivation is the art of getting people to do what you want them to do because they want to do it.

~ Dwight Eisenhower ~

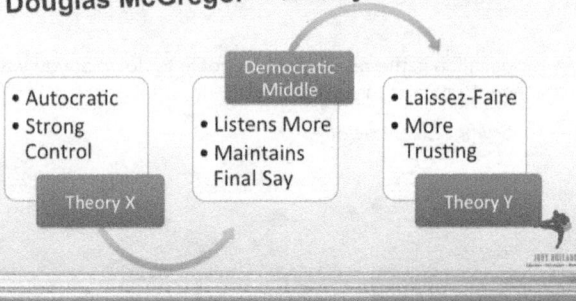

We Manage To Our Apperceptions
Douglas McGregor – Theory X / Theory Y

- Autocratic
- Strong Control

Theory X

Democratic Middle
- Listens More
- Maintains Final Say

- Laissez-Faire
- More Trusting

Theory Y

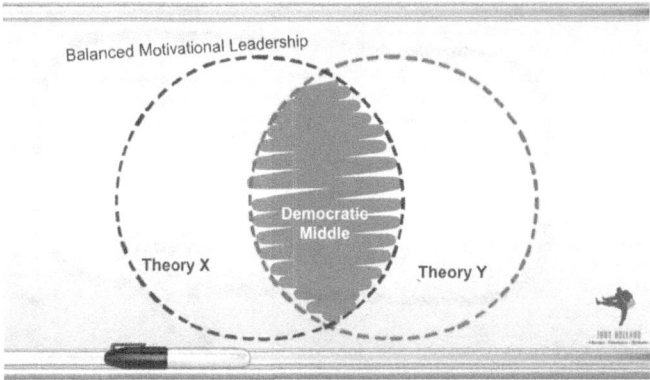

Men wanted for hazardous journey. Small wages, bitter cold, long months of complete darkness, constant danger, safe return doubtful. Honor and recognition in case of success.

-Explorer Ernest Shackleston in a 1890 job ad for the first Antarctic expedition.

WHY WOULD ANYONE VOLUNTEER FOR THIS JOB?

Think about your own experience

- What are the things that drive you to stay motivated?

- What are the things that you have seen work for your team?

Motivation is the driving force behind <u>all actions</u> of human beings.

Motivation is often based on emotions, not factual logic.

We all search for <u>positive emotional</u> experiences and the avoidance of negative ones.

Motivation Is...

- <u>an internal state</u> or condition that activates behavior and gives it direction;

- <u>desire or want</u> that energizes and directs goal-oriented behavior;

- <u>influence</u> of needs and desires on the intensity and direction of behavior.

What is it that employees want?

- To know the organization has purpose and is moving in the right direction
- A good supervisor
- Personal development
- Efficient work systems
- Tools and equipment or to know why not available
- Appreciation
- Good interdepartmental relationships

The numbers are a bit scary at times...

70% of your employees are less motivated today than they used to be.

80% of your employees could perform significantly better if they wanted to (had the emotional desire).

50% of your employees only put enough effort into their work to keep their job.

Statistics are from the book Super Motivation by Dean Spitzer, 1995.

"The only happy people I know are the ones who are working well at something they consider important."

- Abraham H. Maslow

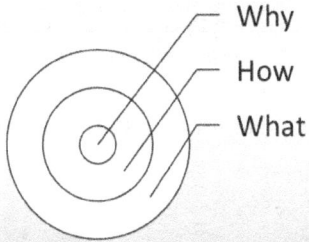

Always Start With Why

- Why
- How
- What

Motivation is everything. You can do the work of
two people, but you can't be two people.
Instead, you have to inspire the next guy down
the line and get him to inspire his people.

~ Lee Iacocca ~

Job Performance Reminder

JP = F (A) (M)

Job Performance = Fit times Ability times Motivation

Anything times zero is zero

What we see depends mainly on what
we look for.

~ John Lubbock ~

10 Tips For Motivating Employees

1. Treat each and every employee with respect.

2. Reward outstanding performance

3. Do not tolerate sustained poor performance

4. Praise accomplishments

5. Celebrate successes and milestones reached

10 Tips For Motivating Employees - Continued

6. Create opportunities for employees to learn & grow

7. Actively listen

8. Clearly communicate goals, responsibilities and expectations

9. Involve employees in plans and decisions

10. Share information

We are what we repeatedly do. Excellence, then, is not an act, but a habit.

~ Aristotle

What Motivates Your Team?

Make a list of three things that
motivate each of your employees.

__ Career Development /
   Success
__ Comfort / Relaxation
__ Health / Balance / Energy
__ Influence / Leadership
__ Learning / Knowledge /
   Discovery
__ Materials/Possessions
__ Recognition/Praise

__ Security/Money/Home
__ Social / Affiliation / Popularity
   / Acceptance
__ Status / Prestige / Stand Out /
   Reputation
__ Task Accomplishment /
   Problem Solving /
   Achievement
__ Teaching / Guiding Others
__ Vitality/Energy
__ Others? _____

Thank You For Your Attention
Check Out
www.jodyholland.com

JODY HOLLAND
· Educates · Entertains · Motivates ·

2 BOOK SUMMARY

Motivation is less about the carrot and the stick and more about the unknown pot of gold at the end of the rainbow. Study after study has shown that it is not the "if-then" statements that matter the most. It is always the "now-that" statements that make the difference. Motivation itself is simply a decision that is made by the person who is to be motivated. Unfortunately, we have built program after program predicated on the idea that throwing something out in front of a person will motivate them to want to do what we want them to do. Here is the simply and yet painful truth. There isn't anything that you can do that will directly motivate another person. That's right. I can't motivate you! You can't motivate me! Now, the second side of that truth is that you can motivate you and I can motivate me. Each of us is in control of our own motivation in this life.

Abraham Maslow, who has been referred to as the "Father of Motivation" explained motivation in terms of a hierarchy. He also said, "If you intentionally become less than you are capable of being, then I warn you; you will be unhappy for the rest of your life." That seemed like an odd statement to me the first time that I read it. I thought, "who in the world would become less than they were capable of being?" Then I thought back to my parents telling me that I could be anything that I wanted to be if I was willing to work at it. I could be president of the United States, or a General in the Army, or an astronaut, or a police officer, or an entrepreneur, or a writer, or literally anything that I wanted to be. The question was... what was I capable of?

In Maslow's Hierarchy of Needs, he describes the five levels as each being dependent on the fulfillment of the previous level. For example, someone who is starving to death is not going to care about self-actualization. In order, Maslow indicated that we must take care of our base needs, such as food and sex. Once our base level needs are taken care of, then and only then can we move to ensuring our own safety. We strive to feel safe physically, mentally, and emotionally. Your brain does not distinguish between types of danger. In fact, you will experience emotional fear in the exact same way as physical fear. This is part of how we can explain the fact that many people have a greater fear of public speaking than they do of drowning. Once we feel safe, we move towards creating social connections. Our social needs include friends and depth in our personal relationships. We need to have people around us that support us, inspire us, challenge us, and help us to move our lives forward. Once we have that, we then are able to truly focus on esteem needs. Our esteem needs will play into both the internal perspective and the external perspective that we have on reality. Achievement and personal success tie into this area. We judge ourselves based on our accomplishments as measure against our beliefs about self. Finally, once we have achieved our definition of success, then we can search of true meaning in life. We begin the self-actualization process, searching for who we are, why we are here, and how we can give back to make the world a better place.

A friend of mine sold one of his companies for a very nice sum of money. He made enough that he would never have to work again. With millions in the bank, he looked me in the eye one day and told me that he had realized that it was never about the money. He wanted to do something that made a difference in the world. I looked him straight in the eye and asked if he would give me all of his money. This caught him off guard and he cocked his head a little, then said, "If I give you all of my money, I would have to work back to this point where life was no longer about money." That statement was full of truth. It was true because it is not about money when you have plenty of it. When you are struggling to make it up the ladder of success and to achieve your definition of success, you are passing through the phases of motivation until you reach self-actualization. Maslow simply said that one must hit each rung on that ladder as they climb their way to the top. We are motivated to move up the ladder of motivation. We are motivated to live into a vision that we have for ourselves. It is just that some people have a clear vision that they pursue and others have a distorted and often wrong vision that they pursue. You will have to decide which is which for you.

The challenging part for many of us is that we have tried to live life without taking proper care of ourselves. We have tried to live as someone that we are not, in the direction that we shouldn't go, for purposes that really aren't ours. When we do that, we live our lives in the misery of no motivation. We live without an inspiring purpose for the actions that we are taking. That doesn't work. It doesn't work because we don't actually want it to work. The only thing that works is what we decide absolutely will work. I think that this explains why people have hobbies and do so much volunteer work. They volunteer to do things that they would pay someone to do at their own house. They do it and they love it and they work their tails off. When I was early in my life, I worked for a non-profit organization. I was responsible for recruiting volunteers, training them, and inspiring them to do great work. One of my duties was in helping to ensure that our camp was funded, fixed, and functional. I had doctors, lawyers, dentists, nurses, teachers, preachers, business owners, and minimum wage employees all working for free to help with plumbing, construction, painting, tree-trimming, and anything else that was needed. In fact, many of them were paying for the chance to work in the heat, without pay, while singing a song, and helping one another. They were extremely motivated and there were no "if-then" statements involved at all.

What I had to understand as an executive was that people loved the opportunity to simply be motivated without any strings attached. They loved the chance to be self-actualized because money was off the table. I think that money itself has hurt motivation more than it has ever helped it. I'm not saying that I want to work for free from this point forward, but I am saying that I work my tail off to do the things that I love to do. I am also saying that I love to write and speak and make a difference in the world. I would do those things regardless of whether I could ever make money at them or not. I am simply blessed that I get to do what I am passionate about and people offer to pay me for it. I wrote and spoke before there was ever money on the table though. I operated on the "now-that" premise. Now-that I have studied for decades and written books and spoken thousands of times, people want to pay me to keep doing what I love to do! That is truly awesome! And, awesome is how I want to live my life.

Below, you will find a variation of Maslow's Hierarchy of needs. It is normally presented in a pyramid format and in the order that I described it earlier. I wanted to make it a little more personable for you, though. So, take a look at the picture and think about how you are fulfilling each of those five areas. Many of us are not really taking care of the top two, or at least not very well. However, they are possible. In fact, other great minds have seen that the order can be reallocated or even rearranged based on a person's values and beliefs.

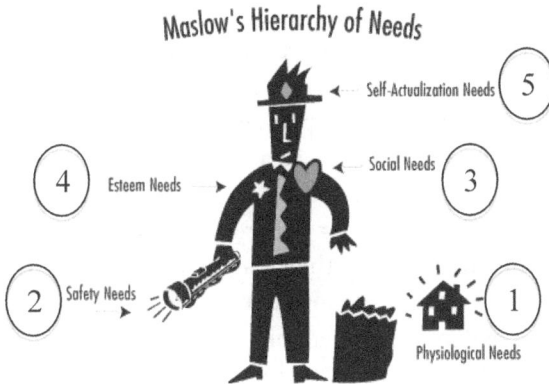

Maslow's Hierarchy of Needs

You have to ask yourself the question… *What motivates me?* For you, it is likely something different than it is for me. The core of society would tell us that we should be motivated by money and power and moving up in the world. What if that wasn't what drove you, though? What if you were driven to help people, like Mother Theresa? What if your calling was to be the best taxi cab driver in your city and that is what you love to do? What if you were designed to stay at home and raise kids? What if you were designed to preach or teach or start businesses? Whatever it is that you were designed to do, you will find that you are only fulfilled when you are doing that thing. I believe that is the reason that other theorists started to realign Maslow's Hierarchy of Needs.

Daniel Pink has written some great works on the science and art of motivation. Pink says that using carrots and sticks is "so last century." It is now more about autonomy, mastery and purpose. (Drive, by Daniel Pink This author could not agree more with what Pink has to say. In fact, as a consultant, this author has seen more top level executives quit their post and move on because of a lack of autonomy, mastery and purpose than for any other reason. Employees at all levels desire the opportunity to participate in directing their career or even their job path. They want a say in what they are doing. They want a challenge that enables them to stretch and grow and become better than they were yesterday. And finally, they want to know that they are making a difference. Adeco, in 2015, indicated on Fox News that more than 80% of people where were employed did not like their job and were disengaged at work. This would indicate that 8 out of every 10 people could produce more at work if they were simply motivated to do so.

Cocktail Party Summary of Drive, as stated by Dan Pink on www.DanPink.com…

COCKTAIL PARTY SUMMARY
When it comes to motivation, there's a gap between what science knows and what business does. Our current business operating system—which is built around external, carrot-and-stick motivators—doesn't work and often does harm. We need an upgrade. And the science shows the way. This new approach has three essential elements: 1. Autonomy – the desire to direct our own lives.

2. Mastery — the urge to get better and better at something that matters.
3. Purpose — the yearning to do what we do in the service of something larger than ourselves.

Pink goes on to say that rewards and incentives work for basic mechanical tasks or physical work. The moment that even rudimentary cognitive skills are required, however, the incentives no longer work. In fact, they have an inverse correlation to performance. Pink looked at research over a 70 year period and discovered that science has known for a very long time that motivation hasn't had anything to do with carrots and sticks in, well, at least the last 7 decades. He clarified that if-then statements work for physical tasks that do not require creative thought. If a person even has to do something as simple as putting together a puzzle, though, the if-then statements no longer work.

Pink goes on to say that what must be employed is the use of now-that statements. When a person is rewarded for something that they already did and they were unaware that a reward was a part of the effort, then the reward garners greater levels of loyalty and motivation. This means that we must be vigilant in watching our people and in appreciating the work that they do as they do it.

So, there are two basic questions that most people want answer to. The first is… What is Motivation? The second is… How do I motivate others?

What is Motivation…

Motivation is a state of focus where an individual chooses to perform at their best and chooses to do more than is asked of them. When a person is motivated, they begin to look for ways to contribute. They willingly give of their talents in order to help their supervisor, their coworkers, their company, society, or some combination of those. Motivation is a feeling as well as a mental construct. According to Zig Ziglar, motivation is preceded by action. According to Steven Pressfield in The War of Art, motivation shows up after the person does. The reality is that motivation is a state of mind that follows a state of action, which was stimulated by a choice to act. The choice to act in the right direction can be a simple one if the conditions for work are right and the skills of the leader are sharp. It can be a very difficult choice to act in the right direction if the supervisors, managers, and/or leaders have not created the right culture.

While it is definitely possible to remain or become motivated with managers and leaders that are not creating the right culture, it is an incredibly self-disciplined choice when the culture is wrong. A great culture can make a mediocre employee strive to be a top performer. A poor or bad culture can make a top performer strive to destroy the success of the company. As leaders, we set the tone for those choice. We make it easy to be motivated or difficult to be motivated. We must accept the responsibility to create the right culture and we must accept responsibility if that culture has not been created thus far.

■■

So How Do You Motivate Others?

I just shared with you that you are responsible for creating the right culture as a leader within your organization. Here comes the tough reality. You cannot directly motivate anyone. People are motivated internally, or intrinsically. There is not magic potion that you can put in the water cooler or the coffee. There is no chant or dance or music that will automatically lead to a motivated staff. You can, however, create a culture where the choice is easy. So, the answer to the question is this… Motivation follows developed and implemented management and leadership skills. As you learn the skills of a great manager and a great leader, and yes they are two different skillsets, then others will simply begin responding to the better culture that you are creating. They will slowly but surely become motivated. They will wake up a little more excited each day to be a part of your team and to make a positive impact.

You motivate others by being motivated, by developing and enhancing your skills on a continuous and never-ending basis, and by being a great manager and leader. People will follow you if you have the skills and implement the skills of someone who is worth following. Please notice that I keep referring to skills and not to titles. People are not motivated to follow you if you are mean, unappreciative, arrogant, intimidating, gruff, unhappy, or even if you have a bigger and fancier title than them.

You create the environment that your employees have to make their choice inside of. It is that environment, that culture, that will ultimately lay the groundwork for the choices that they will make. So, before you lay blame solely on an employee for not being motivated, take a look at the framework within which they make that choice. How you would you choose, honestly, if you were being managed and supervised the way that they are? Put yourself in their shoes and try to see the world the way that they do, with their circumstances, with their reporting structure, with their rules and restrictions. Then, determine what would be best for you to stay motivated if you were in their shoes.

The Law of Reciprocation in Motivation

The law of reciprocation says that when a person receives something, they automatically feel and obligation to return something of equal or greater value, but only when the expectation of reciprocation is not requested by the original giver. Consider the following...

When an employee goes to work for an organization and their supervisor goes out of their way to compliment them on positive behaviors without asking for anything in return, the employee will consistently provide more of the positive behaviors. Additionally, when a supervisor provides a small gift, say an embroidered hat that is not standard, then indicates that they are just excited about their future at the organization, the employee feels a psychological compulsion to prove the supervisor right. The issue only arises when a supervisor provides a gift or a compliment and then follows with, "Now, I expect better performance in return for this."

It is in making the original gift to the employee actually a gift, with no implied obligation, that the obligation is, in fact, made automatic. Perhaps it is in the societal expectations that we have been taught that the secret exists. When we were young, particularly when developing our value structures, we were taught that we are supposed to do something nice for people who are nice to us. We were also taught that there is no such thing as a "free lunch." This implication would indicate that we are obligated to be nice and to return a favor when one is done for us. Rooted in our psychological need for compliance to this unwritten rule of reciprocation, we attempt to equal, and often to out-give the original gift.

There are a number of employees that work extra hours, stay wholly devoted to, and stay loyal to a leader because they are nice. When a supervisor remembers to do things like writing birthday cards, buying presents for the employee's family, etc., then the employee has trouble leaving the organization. To be fully correct, the employee has trouble leaving the supervisor, not really the company. There are so few supervisors that were taught correctly to be nice and respectful that when an employee experiences one, they are both baffled and devoted. In some of my conversations with employees who work for a company that appears to not care about them as a person at all, who remain devoted, I have found that it is their devotion to their direct supervisor, who does care, that keeps them there.

Hawthorne Effect

Workplace conditions were studied at Hawthorne Works in Cicero, Illinois between 1924 and 1932. Elton Mayo was in charge of the research and the research itself was conducted by young male researches. The original intent of the studies was to determine the effects of lighting, as well as other workplace factors, on the overall productivity of factory workers. The idea, by Western Electric, was to determine if increasing lighting in factories would make the workers more productive and more successful on the job. Additionally, they experimented with changing up breaks, break times, work structure itself, and a few other components of work. In typical research fashion, three groups were set up. In one group, the lighting was increased. In another, the lighting remained the same. In the final group, the lighting was actually decreased. The research method involved young men in white coats, interacting with, observing, and taking notes on the work behaviors of the employees. As I stated, it wasn't just the lighting, but the conclusions from the study were fairly consistent regardless of the change that was made.

The overall conclusion was that it was in observing that a temporary positive effect could be accomplished. The act of observation was actually driving behavior more than the changes. If a change was made and no observation was made, the impact was barely noticeable or was negative. If observation happened, with or without change, a positive change happened. The results of the studies were initially labeled as "the observer effect." Henry Landsberger, in reviewing the studies in 1958, dubbed the positive impact that is achieved through simple observation as "The Hawthorne Effect."

This effect can be used incredibly well to influence a team to move in the right direction. For example, when an outside trainer is brought in to teach leadership to all of the supervisors, managers, and the leaders, the entire organization will begin to look for the new leadership characteristics within the participants. This creates a new focus in the workers because they see both hope for better management and a lessening of their focus on what is wrong. This is particularly effective when coupled with an employee survey prior to announcing the new training series that will be implemented. In this case, the survey is implemented and the results reviewed at a high level with the entire staff. Based on the results, the training topics are chosen and then implemented. This provides a level of ownership in the minds of the employees for choosing what direction to take and therefore an obligation to be positive about the direction.

Many times, it is the simple act of changing focus that is needed to spur an employee, or an entire staff, in the right direction. They need to shift their focus in order to see the good that is happening. They become motivated to make it work because, after all, it was their idea.

Holland's Theory of Value-Based Drive

My theory is one of value-based drive. Holland's Theory of Value-Based Drive states…

We are motivated first by creating an image of the world. We assign meaning to everything around us. So, the first tenet of the theory is that nothing has meaning except that which I give it.

The are motivated second by working with people and in a position that fits our definition of the world around us. When we are doing something that we would want to do, even if we didn't get paid, then we have found our fit.

And the third tenet of the theory is that our definition of success must be attainable through the vehicle (work) that we have chosen.

It is fairly easy to tell when people are not living within this motivational model. When a person's labels for reality are wrong, or when they are in the wrong job, or when they realize that they will not achieve their definition of success on the path that they are on, they become demotivated. This misalignment is the cause for a great deal of depression, anger issues, and coping mechanisms. It is also the cause for people living their lives in quiet desperation instead living as fulfilled and happy people.

Over the years, I have had the chance to test the personalities of thousands of people. I have observed their behavioral patterns, which are quite predictable, based on their personality. I have also had the chance to see that people will modify their temperament, or their portrayal of personality to the rest of the world, when they have a shift in values. I have seen that values strongly influence what a person does with their inner drives and feelings. From a simplistic standpoint, we can modify our motivation with some very simple questions.

1. What would I have to believe to be motivated in this situation?
2. Is that something that I can believe if I want to?
3. Do I want to?

I realize that this may sound very simple, but it is incredibly effective in helping you see the world in the image that it needs to be. When you are asking yourself what you would have to believe in order to be motivated, or happy, or driven, or satisfied, or any other emotion, you are asking what the image of the world needs to be in order to achieve the emotional state that you desire.

With the second question, you are then identifying the viability of the belief in your own mind. In James Allen's Book, <u>As A Man Thinketh</u>, he explains that the mind creates your world, not the other way around. He states, "The mind doth make heaven of hell and hell of heaven." It is possible to believe anything if that is what you absolutely choose. The trick is to choose your beliefs so that you live your life the way that you want to live it. You choose motivation by choosing to believe that you are motivated. When you believe that something is possible, then it is possible.

This is simply a question of desire when you get to the third question. Do you want to be motivated? Do you want to believe in the direction that you need to go? Do you want to? When you confidently say, "YES," then it becomes easy to create the right drive in yourself. When you say "NO," then it is virtually impossible to move forward. Everything comes down to creating the image, affirming its possibility, and then choosing it. You are in control.

You can operate in other people's definition of who you should be for a while, but not forever. I have had the chance to meet a number of very unhappy, financially successful people during my life. I have met CEO's that really wanted to be bartenders. I have met CPA's that wanted to be engineers and engineers that wanted to be teachers. The list goes on and on. The point is that when a person tries to live in the image of the world that their parents or their friends or society in general has for them, they are unhappy. They can be disciplined without being motivated. When a person lives their life in the image that fits how they see happiness, then they are happier.

As a caution, there are a number of people that cannot or have not created an image of what the world should be. These are the people that struggle with what reality should be, that self-sabotage, the self-medicate, because they are trying to determine what should be and they are coming up blank. Motivation to succeed stems from believing in a world where they are successful. Never underestimate the power of belief. Belief creates thoughts. Thoughts create actions. Actions create results.

What would you have to believe to love learning about being a great supervisor?

_____

_____

_____

_____

_____

_____

_____

Additional notable theories that you may want to research...

**Clayton Alderfer's ERG Theory (Existence Relatedness and Growth) And the Frustration Regression Principle

**McClelland's Learned Needs (Power, Affiliation, Achievement)

**Herzberg's Two-Factor Theory (Satisfiers versus Dissatisfiers, or Hygiene versus Maintenance)

**Albert Bandura – Self-Efficacy Theory

Notes

ABOUT THE AUTHOR

Jody Holland received his B.A. in Communications from Angelo State University in 1994. He has received specialized training and certifications in physiognomy, conversational hypnosis, team-building, leadership, management, and pre-hire testing. Jody's clients would say that his capacity for creating ROI is what they appreciate the most. He normally gets between a 10X and 25X return on their investment. He has been sought after by clients to speak at their retreats, to assist in changing behaviors in top executives as well as coaching C-Suite leaders for success. Jody has had the opportunity to train and do business in 14 countries and all across the United States. Jody has worked with clients ranging from regional companies to the Fortune 50, including companies like Walmart Corporate, Lockheed Martin, Boeing, and many more. He has worked with First Financial Bancshares, the Community Banker's Association of Illinois, the Illinois Funeral Director's Association, the Illinois State Chamber of Commerce, Leadership Texas, Workforce Development Boards, etc. Jody has been the keynote speaker more than 200 times at conferences and has trained more than 200,000 leaders on topics ranging from generational change at work, to sales, to service, to authentic communication and a variety of other topics focused on interpersonal interactions.

Jody is the author of 12 books, which can be found on Amazon.com, including books on leadership, time management, sales, personal development, and organizational development. Jody has co-authored more than 30 training programs on supervision,

management, leadership, and inter-
generational leadership.

Jody has worked for the State of Texas
modifying the behaviors of former convicts,
designed leadership programs for the Boy
Scouts of America, and successfully built
and sold 3 companies. Jody is a keynote
speaker, author, and trainer… His fun and
witty style of interaction has landed him the
title of Chief Edu-Tainer!

Check out Jody's Website @:
www.JodyHolland.com

Book A Speaker @:
www.OurNextSpeaker.com

Made in United States
Cleveland, OH
24 July 2025